THE KITCHEN LIBRARY

WHOLEFOOD COOKING

THE KITCHEN LIBRARY

WHOLEFOOD COOKING

Carole Handslip

OCTOPUS BOOKS

CONTENTS

NOTES

Standard spoon measurements are used in all recipes
1 tablespoon = one 15 ml spoon
1 teaspoon = one 5 ml spoon
All spoon measures are level.

Ovens should be preheated to the specified temperature.

Use freshly ground black pepper where pepper is specified
and sea salt where salt is stated.

Fresh herbs are used unless otherwise stated. If
unobtainable substitute a bouquet garni of the equivalent
dried herbs, or use dried herbs instead but halve the
quantities stated.

If fresh yeast is unobtainable, substitute dried yeast
but use only half the recommended quantity and follow
the manufacturer's instructions for reconstituting.

For all recipes, quantities are given in both metric and
imperial measures. Follow either set but not a mixture
of both, because they are not interchangeable.

This edition published 1986 by
Octopus Books Limited
59 Grosvenor Street, London W1

© Cathay Books 1981
ISBN 0 7064 2974 5

Printed in Hong Kong

INTRODUCTION

Wholefood cooking is simple and rewarding. It is based on the use of natural ingredients – rich in the vital nutrients to keep you healthy. Wholefood recipes are designed to bring out the full natural flavour of these ingredients, to create tasty, nutritious dishes.

By definition, a wholefood is an unrefined food, to which nothing has been added or taken away. It contains no artificial flavourings, colourings, preservatives or other additives. Essentially, wholefoods are used as close as possible to their original state – to retain their natural flavour and nutrients.

Eating habits have changed quite substantially over the past few centuries. With the development of modern food processing methods, we tend to eat more highly refined foods – particularly sugar, white bread and other refined cereal products. One of the main disadvantages of many processed foods is that they are treated in such a way that the fibre originally present is lost.

Dietary fibre provides the roughage which is essential for the normal working of our digestive systems. Fibre is not broken down during digestion but it encourages other food residues to be eliminated from the body regularly and helps to prevent constipation and other digestive disorders.

In fact, constipation is often an indication that dietary fibre intake needs to be increased. To obtain more fibre, eat plenty of fresh fruit and vegetables, pulses and nuts.

Wholegrains are particularly rich in fibre, so choose whole-meal bread and brown rice in preference to their refined equivalents. Wholemeal flour can normally be used in place of white flour in cooking; it is especially good for pastry.

White sugar is a highly refined food which is used extensively in our modern diet. It provides a quick source of energy but has no other nutritional value and excessive consumption of sugar can promote tooth decay. In fact natural foods, such as vegetables, pulses and grains, can provide all the energy we need in the form of carbohydrate. Fruit contains natural sugar; dried fruit is a particularly good source. To add sweetness to desserts, cakes and biscuits, use natural ingredients – honey, molasses, malt extract and muscovado sugar – rather than white sugar.

Another way of improving our diet is to eat less of those foods which contain saturated fatty acids and cholesterol. Saturated fatty acids, contained in animal fats, such as butter, lard, cream, cheese and meat, tend to raise the blood cholesterol level. An excessively high blood cholesterol level can be a contributory factor in heart disease and blood disorders.

Unsaturated fatty acids, found in vegetable oils, do not raise the blood cholesterol level; it is therefore preferable to use vegetable oils for cooking. The most beneficial oils are those rich in linoleic acid – sunflower, soya, olive and corn oil.

Meat plays a major role in most people's diets. It is, of course, an excellent source of protein, vitamins and minerals, but most types contain a substantial amount of saturated fat.

If used in conjunction with pulses or vegetables, a little meat will provide an economical, nutritious meal. Pulses contain plenty of protein as well as B vitamins and iron.

To flavour savoury dishes, use vegetable stock, unless meat or poultry is the main ingredient. The liquid in which vegetables have been cooked is ideal. For seasoning, choose sea salt or rock salt rather than refined table salt. Both natural salts contain valuable minerals.

The addition of nuts and seeds is often the final touch to make wholefood dishes more interesting, as well as nourishing. They are rich in B vitamins, minerals and proteins, and can be added to cakes and biscuits, sprinkled on breads, or included in salads. When using sesame seeds the flavour is greatly improved by roasting them.

To roast sesame seeds: Place in a heavy based pan over a moderate heat for 3 to 5 minutes until they pop and turn golden brown, shaking the pan constantly.

Sprouting seeds

Mung bean sprouts, or beanshoots as they are usually called, are the most common type of sprouting seeds. However 'sprouts' can be grown easily from all kinds of peas, lentils and beans, as well as alfalfa, fenugreek and cereal grains. They are excellent sources of protein and vitamins.

To sprout seeds: select clean whole seeds and soak in cold water overnight. Drain and place in a large glass jar. Cover the jar with muslin and secure with a rubber band. Two or three times a day, rinse the seeds by pouring cold water through the muslin, then tilting the jar to drain. Most seeds take 4 to 5 days to sprout.

Yogurt and Mint Soup

300 g (10 oz) natural
low-fat yogurt
150 ml ($\frac{1}{4}$ pint) tomato
juice
175 ml (6 fl oz) milk
1 clove garlic, crushed
1 tablespoon chopped
mint
$\frac{1}{2}$ cucumber, peeled
and finely diced
salt and pepper
mint sprigs to garnish

Place the yogurt and tomato juice in a bowl and mix together thoroughly. Stir in the milk, garlic, chopped mint, cucumber and salt and pepper to taste. Transfer to a soup tureen and chill for 2 hours.

Garnish with mint to serve.

Serves 4

Lentil Soup

2 tablespoons oil
1 onion, chopped
1 carrot, chopped
1 celery stick, chopped
1 clove garlic, crushed
125 g (4 oz) lentils
600 ml (1 pint) stock
   or water
salt and pepper
1 tablespoon chopped
   parsley to garnish

Heat the oil in a large pan, add the onion, carrot and celery and fry until softened. Add the remaining ingredients, with salt and pepper to taste. Bring to the boil, cover and simmer for 45 minutes, stirring occasionally. Check the seasoning.

Pour into a warmed tureen and sprinkle with the parsley to serve.
Serves 4

Aduki Bean Soup

125 g (4 oz) aduki
  beans
2 tablespoons oil
1 onion, chopped
1 celery stick, chopped
1 carrot, chopped
1 clove garlic, crushed
2 tomatoes, skinned
  and chopped
1 tablespoon tomato
  purée
1 bay leaf
1 teaspoon chopped
  thyme
900 ml (1½ pints)
  stock or water
salt and pepper
1 tablespoon chopped
  parsley to garnish

Soak the beans in cold water to cover
for 3 hours; drain well.

Heat the oil in a large pan, add the
onion, celery and carrot and cook until
softened. Add the remaining
ingredients, with salt and pepper to
taste. Bring to the boil and simmer for
1 hour.

Pour into a warmed soup tureen and
sprinkle with the parsley to serve.

Serves 4

NOTE: Aduki beans are a small type of
red kidney bean. If unobtainable, use
kidney beans instead.

Hummous

125 g (4 oz) chick
  peas, soaked
  overnight
salt and pepper
2 tablespoons tahini
1–2 cloves garlic,
  crushed
juice of ½ lemon
2 tablespoons olive oil
TO SERVE:
few lettuce leaves
2 teaspoons chopped
  mint

Drain the chick peas, place in a pan and cover with cold water. Bring to the boil and simmer gently for 2 to 2½ hours until soft, adding a little salt towards the end of cooking.

Drain, reserving 120 ml (4 fl oz) of the liquid. Place the chick peas in an electric blender with the tahini, garlic, lemon juice, oil, reserved liquid, ½ teaspoon salt and ¼ teaspoon pepper. Blend to a soft creamy purée; check the seasoning.

Arrange on a bed of lettuce and sprinkle with the mint. Serve with crusty bread.

Serves 4 to 6

Avocado with Green Herb Dressing

2 avocado pears
125 g (4 oz) frozen
  peeled prawns,
  thawed
4 tablespoons Green
  herb dressing
  (see page 63)

Halve the pears and remove the stones.
Scoop out the flesh and cut into neat
pieces. Place in a bowl with the
prawns and dressing.

Mix together carefully and spoon
into individual serving dishes. Serve
with wholemeal bread and butter.
Serves 4

Marinated Kippers

8 kipper fillets,
  fresh or frozen
  and thawed
1 onion, very thinly
  sliced
8 black peppercorns
2 bay leaves
8 tablespoons oil
2 tablespoons cider
  vinegar

Skin the kipper fillets and place in a
shallow earthenware or china dish
with the onion, peppercorns and bay
leaves. Spoon over the oil and vinegar,
cover and leave to marinate for
24 hours, turning once or twice.

Serve chilled with wholemeal bread
and butter.
Serves 4

Aubergine Pâté

2 large aubergines
1 clove garlic, crushed
2 teaspoons lemon
  juice
2 tablespoons olive oil
salt and pepper
2 tablespoons chopped
  parsley
TO GARNISH:
chopped parsley
lemon wedges

Prick the aubergines all over with a
fork, cut in half and place cut side
down on a greased baking sheet. Bake
in a preheated moderately hot oven,
190°C (375°F), Gas Mark 5, for 30 to
40 minutes until softened.

Peel, then blend the aubergines in an
electric blender with the garlic and
lemon juice, adding the oil a teaspoon
at a time. Alternatively, chop the flesh
finely and rub through a sieve, then
add the garlic, lemon juice and oil in a
steady stream, beating until smooth.

Season with salt and pepper to taste,
stir in the parsley and spoon into
ramekin dishes. Chill until required.

Garnish with parsley and lemon
wedges. Serve with wholemeal toast.
Serves 4

Guacamole with Crudités

2 ripe avocado pears
juice of $\frac{1}{2}$ lemon
2 tomatoes, skinned,
   seeded and chopped
$\frac{1}{2}$ small onion, grated
1 clove garlic, crushed
$\frac{1}{2}$ teaspoon Worcestershire sauce
4 tablespoons natural
   low-fat yogurt
salt and pepper
CRUDITÉS:
$\frac{1}{2}$ small cauliflower
4 carrots
4 celery sticks
$\frac{1}{2}$ cucumber
1 green and 1 red
   pepper, cored and
   seeded

Halve the avocados and remove the stones. Scoop the flesh into a bowl and mash with the lemon juice. Add the tomatoes, onion, garlic, Worcestershire sauce, yogurt, and salt and pepper to taste. Beat thoroughly until smooth and turn into a serving dish.

Break the cauliflower into florets and cut the remaining vegetables into matchstick pieces.

Place the dish on a large plate and surround with the vegetables.

Serves 4

Pears with Curd Cheese

50 g (2 oz) Stilton
    cheese
150 g (5 oz) natural
    low-fat yogurt
113 g (4 oz) curd cheese
salt and pepper
2 ripe dessert pears
TO GARNISH:
shredded lettuce leaves
1 tablespoon chopped
    chives

Mash the Stilton cheese with 1 table-spoon of the yogurt and set aside.

Place the curd cheese in a bowl and beat in the remaining yogurt, and salt and pepper to taste.

Peel, halve and core the pears. Place a spoonful of the Stilton filling in each cavity.

Arrange the lettuce on a serving dish and place the pears, cut side down, on top.

Spoon over the yogurt and curd cheese mixture and sprinkle with the chives. Serve chilled.

Serves 4

Butter Bean Vinaigrette

250 g (8 oz) butter
    beans, soaked
    overnight
salt
4 tablespoons
    Vinaigrette dressing
    (see page 64)
4 spring onions,
    chopped
1 clove garlic, crushed
1 tablespoon chopped
    parsley to garnish

Drain the beans, place in a pan and
cover with cold water. Bring to the
boil and simmer gently for 1 to
$1\frac{1}{4}$ hours, adding a little salt towards
the end of cooking; drain.

    Mix with the dressing while the
beans are still warm. Add the onions
and garlic and mix well. Transfer to a
serving dish and leave until cold.
Sprinkle with the parsley to serve.
Serves 4

Melon, Tomato and Grape Vinaigrette

2 small ogen melons
4 tomatoes, skinned,
    quartered and seeded
175 g (6 oz) black
    grapes, halved and
    seeded
4 tablespoons Mint and
    honey dressing (see
    page 64)
1 tablespoon sesame
    seeds, roasted
4 mint sprigs to garnish

Cut the melons in half and discard the seeds. Scoop the flesh into balls, using a melon baller, or cut into cubes; reserve the shells. Place the melon in a bowl with the tomatoes and grapes. Pour over the dressing.

Toss well, then spoon the mixture into the melon shells. Sprinkle with the sesame seeds and garnish with the mint to serve.
Serves 4

EGG & CHEESE DISHES

Eggs Flamenco

4 tablespoons olive oil
1 onion, chopped
2 red peppers, cored,
   seeded and cut into
   strips
175 g (6 oz) piece
   smoked streaky
   bacon, derinded and
   cut into strips
2 potatoes, boiled and
   diced
125 g (4 oz) shelled
   fresh or frozen peas
4 tomatoes, skinned
   and chopped
1 tablespoon chopped
   parsley
salt and pepper
4 eggs

Heat the oil in a pan, add the onion, peppers and bacon and fry for 5 to 6 minutes. Add the potatoes and cook until lightly browned. Add the peas, tomatoes, parsley, and salt and pepper to taste. Cook gently for 10 minutes, adding a little water if necessary to prevent the mixture sticking.

Turn the vegetable mixture into a greased shallow ovenproof dish. Make 4 hollows in the mixture and break an egg into each one. Cook in a preheated moderate oven, 180°C (350°F), Gas Mark 4, for 15 minutes until the egg whites are just set. Serve immediately.
Serves 4

Spinach Omelet

40 g (1½ oz) margarine
   or butter
250 g (8 oz) spinach,
   finely chopped
1 tablespoon natural
   low-fat yogurt
grated nutmeg
salt and pepper
4 eggs

Melt 25 g (1 oz) of the fat in a pan.
Add the spinach and cook over a gentle
heat for 4 to 5 minutes, stirring
occasionally. Remove from the heat
and stir in the yogurt. Season with
nutmeg, salt and pepper to taste and
keep hot.

Beat the eggs in a bowl, with salt and
pepper to taste. Melt the remaining fat
in a 28 cm (10 inch) omelet pan.
When the butter is foaming, pour in
the eggs. When the omelet begins to
set, lift the cooked edge to allow the
unset egg to run onto the pan.

Place the filling in the centre of the
omelet, cook for 1 minute then fold in
half. Slide onto a warmed plate and
serve immediately.
Serves 2

Spinach Roulade

500 g (1 lb) spinach
4 eggs, separated
salt and pepper
grated nutmeg
FILLING:
2 tablespoons oil
1 onion, chopped
175 g (6 oz) mush-
  rooms, sliced
1 tablespoon wholemeal
  flour
150 ml (¼ pint) milk
1 tablespoon grated
  Parmesan cheese

Cook the spinach in a large pan with just the water clinging to the leaves after washing, for 5 minutes. Drain thoroughly and chop finely.

Place in a bowl with the egg yolks, and salt, pepper and nutmeg to taste; mix well. Whisk the egg whites until stiff and fold into the mixture.

Spread the mixture evenly in a lined and greased 30 × 20 cm (12 × 8 inch) Swiss roll tin. Cook in a preheated moderately hot oven, 200°C (400°F), Gas Mark 6, for 10 to 15 minutes until risen and firm.

Heat the oil in a pan, add the onion and fry until soft. Add the mushrooms and fry for 2 to 3 minutes. Stir in the flour, then gradually stir in the milk. Add salt and pepper to taste and simmer for 2 to 3 minutes.

Sprinkle the cheese over a sheet of greaseproof paper. Turn the roulade out onto the paper and peel off the lining paper. Spread with the filling and roll up like a Swiss roll.

Serve immediately.
Serves 4

Piperade

2 tablespoons oil
1 large onion, sliced
1 red and 1 green
  pepper, cored, seeded
  and sliced
2 cloves garlic, crushed
4 tomatoes, skinned
  and chopped
salt and pepper
4 eggs, beaten with
  2 tablespoons milk

Heat the oil in a pan, add the onion and peppers and fry until softened. Add the garlic, tomatoes, and salt and pepper to taste. Simmer for 5 minutes, pour in the eggs and cook for 3 to 4 minutes, stirring occasionally.

Turn onto a warmed dish and serve immediately with crusty bread and a green salad.
Serves 2

Cheese and Herb Mousse

350 g (12 oz) cottage
  cheese, sieved
½ cucumber, peeled
  and diced
1 tablespoon chopped
  parsley
1 tablespoon chopped
  chives
1 tablespoon chopped
  thyme
salt and pepper
15 g (½ oz) gelatine,
  soaked in 3 table-
  spoons cold water
150 ml (¼ pint)
  Mayonnaise (see
  page 62)
watercress to garnish

Put the cottage cheese in a bowl with
the cucumber, herbs, and salt and
pepper to taste; mix well.

Place the soaked gelatine in a bowl
over a pan of simmering water and stir
until dissolved. Cool slightly, then
stir into the cheese mixture with the
mayonnaise.

Turn into a greased 750 ml (1¼ pint)
ring mould and leave to set in the
refrigerator.

Turn out onto a serving dish and
garnish with watercress to serve.
Serves 6

Spinach and Cheese Flan

WHOLEMEAL PASTRY:
150 g (6 oz) whole-
  meal flour
pinch of salt
75 g (3 oz) margarine
  or butter
2–3 tablespoons water
FILLING:
500 g (1 lb) spinach
salt and pepper
227 g (8 oz) cottage
  cheese
2 eggs
50 g (2 oz) Parmesan
  cheese, grated
150 ml (¼ pint) milk
grated nutmeg

Place the flour and salt in a mixing
bowl and rub in the margarine or
butter until the mixture resembles
breadcrumbs. Add the water and
mix to a firm dough, then turn onto a
floured surface and knead lightly until
smooth. Roll out thinly and use to line
a 20 cm (8 inch) flan ring placed on a
baking sheet. Chill for 15 minutes.

Meanwhile, prepare the filling. Put
the spinach in a large pan with just the
water clinging to the leaves after
washing and a pinch of salt. Cook
gently for 5 minutes, turning twice.
Drain thoroughly and chop finely.
Place in a bowl with the remaining
ingredients, seasoning with salt, pepper
and nutmeg to taste. Mix thoroughly.

Pour into the flan case, smooth the
top and bake in a preheated moderately
hot oven, 190°C (375°F), Gas Mark 5,
for 35 to 40 minutes. Serve hot or cold.
Serves 4

Pepper Quiche

CHEESE PASTRY:
150 g (6 oz) whole-meal flour
½ teaspoon dry mustard
pinch of salt
pinch of cayenne pepper
75 g (3 oz) margarine
75 g (3 oz) Cheddar cheese, grated
2–3 tablespoons water

FILLING:
2 tablespoons oil
1 onion, chopped
1 clove garlic, crushed
1 green and 1 red pepper, cored, seeded and sliced
2 eggs
150 ml (¼ pint) milk
50 g (2 oz) wholemeal breadcrumbs
salt and pepper

Place the flour, mustard, salt and cayenne pepper in a mixing bowl. Rub in the margarine until the mixture resembles breadcrumbs. Stir in the cheese, add the water and mix to a firm dough. Turn onto a floured surface and knead lightly until smooth. Roll out thinly and use to line a 23 cm (9 inch) flan ring placed on a baking sheet. Chill for 15 minutes.

Meanwhile, heat the oil in a pan, add the onion and fry until softened. Add the garlic and peppers and cook for 10 minutes. Mix the eggs and milk together, then stir in the pepper mixture, breadcrumbs, and salt and pepper to taste.

Pour into the flan case and bake in a preheated moderately hot oven, 190°C (375°F), Gas Mark 5, for 35 to 40 minutes until golden. Serve hot or cold, with salad.
Serves 4

Wholemeal Pizza

DOUGH:
250 g (8 oz) whole-
    meal flour
$\frac{1}{2}$ teaspoon salt
7 g ($\frac{1}{4}$ oz) fresh yeast
150 ml ($\frac{1}{4}$ pint) warm
    water
1 tablespoon olive oil
TOPPING:
1 tablespoon olive oil
1 large onion, sliced
500 g (1 lb) tomatoes,
    skinned and chopped
1 tablespoon chopped
    marjoram
salt and pepper
2 tablespoons tomato
    purée
250 g (8 oz)
    Mozzarella or Bel
    Paese cheese, thinly
    sliced
1 × 49 g ($1\frac{3}{4}$ oz) can
    anchovy fillets,
    halved lengthways
8 black olives, halved
    and stoned

Mix the flour and salt together in a
bowl. Cream the yeast with a little of
the water and leave until frothy. Add
to the flour with the remaining water
and the oil and mix to a soft dough.

Turn onto a floured surface and
knead for 10 minutes until smooth and
elastic. Place in a clean bowl, cover
with a damp cloth and leave to rise in
a warm place for about $1\frac{1}{2}$ hours, until
doubled in size.

Meanwhile, heat the oil in a pan, add
the onion and fry until softened. Add
the tomatoes, marjoram, and salt and
pepper to taste and cook for 5 minutes.

Turn the dough onto a floured
surface and knead for a few minutes.
Divide in half and roll each piece out
to a 20 cm (8 inch) circle. Place on
greased baking sheets and spread with
the tomato purée. Spoon over the
tomato mixture and cover with the
cheese. Top with the anchovies and
olives.

Bake in a preheated moderately hot
oven, 200°C (400°F), Gas Mark 6, for
15 to 20 minutes. Serve immediately.
Serves 4

Cheese and Onion Oat Flan

OAT PASTRY:
125 g (4 oz) whole-
meal flour
125 g (4 oz) medium
oatmeal
pinch of salt
125 g (4 oz) margarine
2–3 tablespoons water
FILLING:
2 tablespoons oil
2 onions, chopped
2 eggs
150 ml ($\frac{1}{4}$ pint) milk
250 g (8 oz) Cheddar
cheese, grated
salt and pepper

Place the flour, oatmeal and salt in a
mixing bowl and rub in the margarine
until the mixture resembles breadcrumbs. Add the water and mix to a
firm dough. Turn onto a floured
surface and knead lightly until smooth.
Roll out and use to line a 20 cm
(8 inch) flan dish. Chill for 15 minutes.

Meanwhile, make the filling. Heat
the oil in a pan, add the onions and
fry gently until transparent. Mix the
eggs and milk together, then stir in the
cheese, onions, and salt and pepper to
taste.

Pour into the flan case and bake in a
preheated moderately hot oven, 190°C
(375°F), Gas Mark 5, for 35 to 40
minutes. Serve hot or cold, with salad.
Serves 4

Chicken with Honey

3 tablespoons clear
  honey
1 teaspoon dry
  mustard
1 teaspoon salt
$\frac{1}{2}$ teaspoon pepper
2 teaspoons soy sauce
1 × 1.5 kg (3 lb) oven-
  ready chicken
150 ml ($\frac{1}{4}$ pint)
  chicken stock
150 ml ($\frac{1}{4}$ pint) white
  wine
125 g (4 oz) green
  grapes, halved and
  seeded
150 g (5 oz) natural
  low-fat yogurt

Place the honey, mustard, salt, pepper and soy sauce in a small basin and mix well. Spread the mixture over the chicken, place in a roasting pan and pour in the stock.

Roast in a preheated moderately hot oven, 200°C (400°F), Gas Mark 6, for 1 to 1$\frac{1}{4}$ hours, basting occasionally. Carve and arrange on a warmed serving dish; keep hot.

Pour the wine into the roasting pan and stir to mix in the juices. Bring to the boil, add the grapes and check the seasoning. Stir in the yogurt. Pour over the chicken to serve.

Serves 4

Poussins with Herb Sauce

2 tablespoons oil
4 × 400 g (14 oz)
    poussins (young
    chicken)
grated rind and juice
    of 1 lemon
2 tablespoons chicken
    stock
salt and pepper
2 tablespoons chopped
    mixed herbs (parsley,
    chives, thyme and
    marjoram)
150 ml (¼ pint) double
    cream
watercress to garnish

Heat the oil in a large pan, add the
poussins and brown lightly all over.
Add the lemon rind and juice, stock,
and salt and pepper to taste.

Cover and simmer for 20 to 25
minutes until tender. Place on a
warmed serving dish and keep hot.

Add the herbs and cream to the pan
and heat gently. Check the seasoning.
Pour the sauce around the poussins and
garnish with watercress to serve.
Serves 4

Bacon and Nut Ring

2 tablespoons oil
1 onion, chopped
1 clove garlic, crushed
125 g (4 oz) streaky
   bacon, derinded and
   chopped
2 celery sticks,
   chopped
1 tablespoon wholemeal
   flour
175 ml (6 fl oz)
   tomato juice
125 g (4 oz) whole-
   meal breadcrumbs
125 g (4 oz) hazelnuts,
   coarsely ground
1 tablespoon rolled
   oats
1 tablespoon chopped
   parsley
1 egg, beaten
salt and pepper
watercress to garnish

Heat the oil in a pan, add the onion, garlic, bacon and celery and fry for 4 minutes until softened. Mix in the flour, then add the tomato juice, stirring until the mixture thickens. Add the remaining ingredients, seasoning with $\frac{1}{2}$ teaspoon salt and pepper to taste. Mix thoroughly.

Press the mixture into a greased 19 cm ($7\frac{1}{2}$ inch) ring mould and cover with foil. Cook in a preheated moderate oven, 180°C (350°F), Gas Mark 4, for 1 hour.

Turn out onto a warmed serving dish, garnish with watercress and serve hot with tomato sauce (see page 49). Alternatively, serve cold with salad.

Serves 4

NOTE: For a vegetarian dish, replace the bacon with grated cheese.

28

Chicken and Mushroom Pie

PASTRY:

250 g (8 oz) whole-
    meal flour
pinch of salt
125 g (4 oz) margarine
    or butter
2–3 tablespoons water
beaten egg to glaze

FILLING:

2 tablespoons oil
1 onion, chopped
1 clove garlic, crushed
125 g (4 oz)
    mushrooms, sliced
1 tablespoon wholemeal
    flour
300 ml ($\frac{1}{2}$ pint)
    chicken stock
500 g (1 lb) cooked
    chicken, diced
1 tablespoon chopped
    parsley
salt and pepper

Make the pastry as for Spinach and
cheese flan (see page 22); chill for
15 minutes.

Meanwhile, heat the oil in a pan,
add the onion and fry until softened.
Add the garlic and mushrooms and
cook for 2 minutes. Remove from the
heat and stir in the flour; add the stock
and stir until blended. Return to the
heat and bring to the boil, stirring
until thickened. Add the remaining
ingredients, with salt and pepper to
taste. Mix well, then transfer to a
1.2 litre (2 pint) pie dish.

Roll out the pastry to a shape about
5 cm (2 inches) larger than the dish.
Cut off a narrow strip all round and
place on the dampened edge of the
dish. Moisten the strip, then cover with
the pastry, pressing the edges firmly.

Trim and flute the edges, decorate
with pastry leaves made from the
trimmings, and make a hole in the
centre. Brush with beaten egg and bake
in a preheated moderately hot oven,
200°C (400°F), Gas Mark 6, for
30 minutes until golden. Serve hot.

Serves 4

Kidney and Bacon Kebabs

12 rashers streaky
    bacon, derinded
2 green peppers,
    cored and seeded
12 lambs' kidneys
6 small onions
2 tablespoons olive oil
1 tablespoon thyme
    leaves
PILAF:
2 tablespoons olive oil
1 onion, chopped
1 red pepper, cored,
    seeded and chopped
1 clove garlic, crushed
250 g (8 oz) brown
    rice
600 ml (1 pint) stock
1 bay leaf
salt and pepper
50 g (2 oz) raisins
TO FINISH:
2 tablespoons soy sauce
2 tablespoons chopped
    parsley

First, prepare the pilaf. Heat the oil
in a pan, add the onion and cook until
softened. Add the pepper, garlic and
rice and cook for a further 2 minutes,
stirring. Add the stock, bay leaf, and
salt and pepper to taste. Bring to the
boil, stirring occasionally, cover and
simmer for 35 minutes. Add the raisins
and cook for a further 5 to 10 minutes
until the stock is absorbed.

Cut the bacon rashers in half and roll
up. Cut the peppers into 24 pieces.
Skin, core and halve the kidneys.
Cut the onions into quarters.

Thread the kidney, bacon, onion and
pepper alternately onto 8 skewers. Mix
the oil and thyme with $\frac{1}{2}$ teaspoon salt
and $\frac{1}{4}$ teaspoon pepper; brush over the
kebabs. Cook under a preheated hot
grill for 8 to 10 minutes, turning and
basting with the oil mixture frequently.

Stir the soy sauce and parsley into
the pilaf. Turn onto a warmed serving
dish and arrange the kebabs on top.
Serves 4

Liver with Herbs

2 tablespoons whole-
    meal flour
salt and pepper
500 g (1 lb) lambs'
    liver, sliced
2 tablespoons oil
2 onions, chopped
150 ml ($\frac{1}{4}$ pint) red
    wine
150 ml ($\frac{1}{4}$ pint) stock
2 tablespoons tomato
    purée
1 teaspoon chopped
    thyme
2 tomatoes, skinned,
    seeded and sliced
1 tablespoon chopped
    parsley to garnish

Season the flour with salt and pepper
and use to coat the liver. Heat the
oil in a pan, add the liver and fry
gently for 2 minutes on each side.
Remove from the pan and keep hot.

Add the onions to the pan and fry
gently until softened. Stir in the wine,
stock, tomato purée, thyme, and salt
and pepper to taste. Bring to the boil.
Return the liver to the pan, cover and
simmer for 15 minutes. Add the
tomatoes and cook for a further
5 minutes or until the liver is tender.

Arrange the liver on a warmed
serving dish. Pour the sauce over the
liver. Sprinkle with parsley and
serve immediately.
Serves 4

Lamb Cutlets Provençale

4 tablespoons whole-
    meal breadcrumbs
1 teaspoon salt
½ teaspoon pepper
8 lamb cutlets,
    trimmed
1 egg, beaten
oil for shallow frying
PROVENÇALE SAUCE:
2 tablespoons olive oil
1 onion, sliced
1 red and 1 green
    pepper, cored, seeded
    and sliced
4 tomatoes, skinned
1 clove garlic, crushed
1 teaspoon tomato
    purée
1 teaspoon chopped
    thyme
salt and pepper
TO GARNISH:
1 tablespoon chopped
    parsley

Mix the breadcrumbs with the salt and pepper. Brush the cutlets with the egg and roll in the breadcrumbs, pressing on well with a palette knife.

To make the sauce: heat the oil in a pan, add the onion and peppers and fry until softened. Cut the tomatoes into eighths and add to the pan. Add the remaining ingredients, with salt and pepper to taste. Cover and simmer for 7 to 8 minutes.

Pour the oil into a frying pan to a depth of 5 mm (¼ inch) and place over moderate heat. When the oil is hot, add the chops and fry for 4 to 5 minutes on each side until tender and golden brown; drain on kitchen paper.

Arrange the cutlets along one side of a warmed serving dish and spoon the sauce on the other side. Sprinkle with the parsley and serve with brown rice.
Serves 4

Cassoulet Toulousain

750 g (1½ lb) haricot
  beans, soaked
  overnight
1 large onion, chopped
4 cloves garlic, chopped
350 g (12 oz) piece
  smoked collar bacon
1 bouquet garni
2 duckling portions
500 g (1 lb) belly
  pork
250 g (8 oz) piece
  garlic sausage
500 g (1 lb) tomatoes,
  skinned and
  chopped
salt and pepper
50 g (2 oz) wholemeal
  breadcrumbs

Drain the beans, place in a large pan
and cover with cold water. Add the
onion, garlic, bacon and herbs. Bring
to the boil and simmer for 1½ hours.
Drain the beans, reserving the liquid,
and remove the bacon.

Place the duckling and pork on a
rack in a roasting pan and roast in a
preheated moderately hot oven, 200°C
(400°F), Gas Mark 6, for 1 hour.

Cut the bacon, duckling, pork and
sausage into pieces. Arrange the meats
in a deep earthenware casserole in
alternate layers with the beans and
tomatoes; season each layer with salt
and pepper to taste. Pour in enough of
the reserved liquid to come halfway up
the casserole. Cover and cook in a
preheated moderate oven, 160°C
(325°F), Gas Mark 3, for 1½ hours.

Remove the lid, add a little more
liquid if necessary and sprinkle over
the breadcrumbs. Return to the oven
for 1 to 1½ hours until a thick golden
crust has formed.

Serve with a green salad.

Serves 6 to 8

Black Bean Casserole

350 g (12 oz) black
   beans, soaked
   overnight
2 tablespoons olive oil
2 onions, sliced
2 celery sticks, sliced
2 carrots, sliced
2 cloves garlic, crushed
500 g (1 lb)
   frankfurter sausages,
   thickly sliced
1 tablespoon tomato
   purée
1 bay leaf
500 g (1 lb) tomatoes,
   skinned and chopped
salt and pepper
1 tablespoon chopped
   parsley to garnish

Drain the beans, place in a pan and cover with cold water. Bring to the boil and simmer gently for 1 hour. Drain and reserve 450 ml ($\frac{3}{4}$ pint) of the liquid.

Heat the oil in a flameproof casserole, add the onions and fry for 5 to 10 minutes until transparent. Add the celery, carrots and garlic and fry for 3 to 4 minutes.

Add the remaining ingredients, with the beans, reserved liquid, and salt and pepper to taste. Cover and cook in a preheated moderate oven, 180°C (350°F), Gas Mark 4, for 1 to 1$\frac{1}{2}$ hours until the beans are soft. Sprinkle with the parsley and serve immediately.
Serves 4

Puchero

350 g (12 oz) pinto
   beans, soaked
   overnight
250 g (8 oz) salt pork
2 tablespoons olive oil
1 large onion, sliced
1 red and 1 green
   pepper, cored,
   seeded and sliced
2 cloves garlic, crushed
2 teaspoons tomato
   purée
4 tomatoes, skinned
   and quartered
250 g (8 oz) chorizo
   or garlic sausage,
   thickly sliced
salt and pepper
1 tablespoon chopped
   parsley

Drain the beans, place in a pan and cover with cold water. Bring to the boil and simmer for 50 to 60 minutes. Drain and reserve 450 ml ($\frac{3}{4}$ pint) of the liquid.

Cover the pork with cold water, bring to the boil and simmer for 30 minutes. Drain and cut into chunks.

Heat the oil in a pan, add the onion and peppers and fry for 8 to 10 minutes until softened. Add the garlic, tomato purée, pork pieces, beans and the reserved liquid. Bring to the boil and simmer for 1 hour. Add the tomatoes, chorizo or garlic sausage, and salt and pepper to taste. Cook for a further 30 minutes.

Turn into a warmed dish and sprinkle with the parsley to serve.
Serves 4 to 6

Trout with Herbs

4 tablespoons whole-
    meal flour
½ teaspoon salt
¼ teaspoon pepper
4 trout, cleaned
3 tablespoons oil
TO FINISH:
25 g (1 oz) butter
juice of ½ lemon
1 tablespoon chopped
    mixed herbs
    (parsley, chives and
    thyme)
salt and pepper

Mix together the flour, salt and pepper and use to coat the trout. Heat the oil in a heavy frying pan, add the fish and fry for 5 to 6 minutes on each side until golden brown. Place on a warmed serving dish and keep hot.

Wipe the frying pan with kitchen paper. Add the butter and cook until golden brown. Quickly add the lemon juice, herbs, and salt and pepper to taste. Pour over the trout and serve immediately.

Serves 4

Scandinavian Mackerel

3 tablespoons cider
  vinegar
300 ml (½ pint) water
1 onion, sliced
1 bay leaf
1 parsley sprig
1 thyme sprig
6 peppercorns
½ teaspoon salt
4 mackerel, cleaned
SAUCE:
150 g (5 oz) natural
  low-fat yogurt
1 tablespoon French
  mustard
1 teaspoon muscovado
  sugar
1 tablespoon cider
  vinegar
1 tablespoon chopped
  fennel
TO GARNISH:
lemon wedges

Put the vinegar, water, onion, herbs, peppercorns and salt in a pan. Bring to the boil and simmer for 20 minutes.

Place the mackerel in a shallow ovenproof dish and pour over the infused liquid. Cover and cook in a preheated moderate oven, 180°C (350°F), Gas Mark 4, for 20 to 25 minutes. Transfer the fish to a warmed serving dish and keep hot.

Put all the sauce ingredients in a small bowl and place over a pan of simmering water. Stir until blended and heated through.

Pour over the fish, garnish with lemon wedges and serve immediately.
Serves 4

ILLUSTRATED BELOW: Preparing Scandinavian mackerel for cooking.

Soused Herrings

150 ml (¼ pint) white
  wine vinegar
150 ml (¼ pint) white
  wine
150 ml (¼ pint) water
1 tablespoon pickling
  spice
8 peppercorns
1 bay leaf
1 onion, thinly sliced
1 teaspoon salt
1 tablespoon muscovado
  sugar
6 boned herrings

Put all the ingredients, except the fish,
into a pan. Bring to the boil then leave
to cool.

Place the herrings in a shallow ovenproof dish and pour over the liquid.
Cover and cook in a preheated
moderate oven, 160°C (325°F), Gas
Mark 3, for 1 hour. Allow to cool,
then chill in the refrigerator overnight.

Serve with salad and crusty
wholemeal bread.

Serves 6

Smoked Haddock Crêpes

PANCAKE BATTER:
125 g (4 oz) whole-
  meal flour
1 egg, beaten
300 ml (½ pint) milk
1 tablespoon oil
FILLING:
500 g (1 lb) smoked
  haddock fillets
300 ml (½ pint) milk
40 g (1½ oz) margarine
40 g (1½ oz)
  wholemeal flour
2 hard-boiled eggs,
  chopped
salt and pepper
25 g (1 oz) butter,
  melted
25 g (1 oz) grated
  Parmesan cheese

Make and cook the crêpes as for
Spinach pancake layer (see page 44).

Place the haddock in a pan, add the
milk, cover and bring to the boil.
Simmer for 5 minutes. Leave the fish
to cool slightly in the pan, then lift out
with a fish slice. Remove the skin and
flake, discarding any bones. Strain the
liquid and make up to 300 ml (½ pint)
with extra milk if necessary; keep on
one side.

Melt the margarine in a pan, remove
from the heat and stir in the flour.
Pour in the reserved liquid and stir
until blended. Return to the heat and
bring to the boil, stirring, until
thickened. Add the eggs, fish, and salt
and pepper to taste.

Place a spoonful of filling on each
crêpe, roll up and place in an oiled
shallow ovenproof dish. Brush with the
melted butter and sprinkle with the
Parmesan cheese. Cook in a preheated
moderately hot oven, 190°C (375°F),
Gas Mark 5, for 15 minutes until crisp.
Serve immediately.

Serves 4 to 6

Mediterranean Fish Stew

3 tablespoons olive
   oil
2 onions, sliced
2 cloves garlic, crushed
4 large tomatoes,
   skinned and chopped
150 ml ($\frac{1}{4}$ pint) water
150 ml ($\frac{1}{4}$ pint) white
   wine
1 bay leaf
1 teaspoon salt
$\frac{1}{2}$ teaspoon pepper
750 g (1$\frac{1}{2}$ lb) cod
   fillet, skinned and
   boned
600 ml (1 pint) mussels
175 g (6 oz) frozen
   peeled prawns,
   thawed
1 tablespoon chopped
   parsley

Heat the oil in a pan, add the onions
and fry until softened. Add the garlic,
tomatoes, half the water, the wine, bay
leaf, salt and pepper. Simmer for
15 minutes.

Cut the cod into 5 cm (2 inch)
squares, add to the pan and simmer for
15 minutes.

Scrub the mussels thoroughly, pulling
off the beard. Discard any which are
open and will not close when tapped.
Put them into a heavy pan with the
remaining water, cover and cook over
a high heat for 5 minutes until they
have opened; discard any that do not.

Discard the top shell from each
mussel. Add the mussels with their
liquid and the prawns to the stew.
Cook for a further 3 minutes.

Turn into a warmed serving dish and
sprinkle with the parsley. Serve with
crusty wholemeal bread.
Serves 4 to 6

Prawn Risotto

4 tablespoons oil
1 onion, chopped
250 g (8 oz) brown
   rice
600 ml (1 pint) water
salt and pepper
1 red pepper, cored,
   seeded and chopped
1 clove garlic, crushed
50 g (2 oz) flaked
   almonds
350 g (12 oz) frozen
   peeled prawns,
   thawed
1 tablespoon chopped
   parsley

Heat half the oil in a pan, add the
onion and fry until softened. Add the
rice and cook for 2 minutes, stirring.
Add the water and 1 teaspoon salt and
bring to the boil. Simmer for 40 to
45 minutes, adding more water if
necessary.

Heat the remaining oil in a pan, add
the pepper and fry for 3 minutes. Add
the garlic, almonds and prawns. Fry
for a further 2 minutes, until the
almonds are browned and the prawns
heated through.

Stir into the cooked rice, add pepper
to taste and more salt if necessary.
Transfer to a warmed dish and sprinkle
with the parsley.
Serves 4

Cod in Tomato Sauce

4 cod steaks, fresh
  or frozen
TOMATO SAUCE:
4 tablespoons olive oil
500 g (1 lb) tomatoes,
  skinned and chopped
1 clove garlic, crushed
1 tablespoon chopped
  parsley
4 tablespoons white
  wine
salt and pepper

First make the tomato sauce. Heat the oil in a pan, add the tomatoes, garlic, parsley, wine, and salt and pepper to taste. Simmer for 7 to 10 minutes, stirring occasionally.

Pour half the sauce into a shallow casserole dish, lay the fish on top and cover with the remaining sauce. Cover and cook in a preheated moderately hot oven, 190°C (375°F), Gas Mark 5, for 20 to 25 minutes until cooked. Turn onto a warmed dish and serve immediately.
Serves 4

Spiced Cauliflower

2 tablespoons oil
1 teaspoon ground
  ginger
2 teaspoons ground
  coriander
1 teaspoon ground
  turmeric
1 cauliflower, broken
  into florets
2 carrots, thinly sliced
1 onion, sliced
2 celery sticks, sliced
120 ml (4 fl oz) stock
salt and pepper
150 g (5 oz) natural
  low-fat yogurt
1 tablespoon chopped
  coriander or parsley

Heat the oil in a pan, add the spices
and fry gently for 1 minute. Add the
vegetables and cook gently for a
further 3 minutes, stirring occasionally.
Add the stock, and salt and pepper to
taste.

Cover and simmer for 10 minutes
until the vegetables are just tender.
Stir in the yogurt, sprinkle with the
coriander or parsley and serve
immediately.
Serves 4

Stir-Fried Vegetables

2 tablespoons oil
1 large onion, sliced
2 carrots, cut into
    thin strips
2 celery sticks, sliced
1 green pepper, cored,
    seeded and sliced
2 teaspoons chopped
    root ginger
125 g (4 oz)
    mushrooms, sliced
250 g (8 oz) bean-
    shoots
1 clove garlic, crushed
2 tablespoons sherry
2 tablespoons soy sauce
salt and pepper

Heat the oil in a wok or deep frying pan. Add the onion, carrots, celery, pepper and ginger and fry briskly for 5 minutes, stirring constantly.

Add the mushrooms, beanshoots and garlic and stir-fry for a further 2 minutes.

Add the sherry, soy sauce, and salt and pepper to taste. Stir-fry for about 3 minutes.

Serve immediately.

Serves 4

Spinach Pancake Layer

PANCAKE BATTER:
125 g (4 oz) whole-
    meal flour
1 egg, beaten
300 ml (½ pint) milk
1 tablespoon oil
FILLING:
750 g (1½ lb) spinach
salt and pepper
227 g (8 oz) cottage
    cheese
1 egg, beaten
grated nutmeg
TO FINISH:
50 g (2 oz) Cheddar
    cheese, grated

Place the flour in a bowl and make a well in the centre. Add the egg, then gradually stir in half the milk and the oil. Beat thoroughly until smooth. Add the remaining milk.

Heat a 15 cm (6 inch) omelet pan and add a few drops of oil. Pour in 1 tablespoon of the batter and tilt the pan to coat the bottom evenly. Cook until the underside is brown, then turn over and cook for a further 10 seconds. Turn onto a warmed plate. Repeat with the remaining batter, making 12 pancakes. Stack, interleaved with greaseproof paper as they are cooked; keep warm.

Cook the spinach in a large pan with just the water clinging to the leaves after washing and a pinch of salt for 5 minutes; drain thoroughly. Chop finely and put in a bowl. Add the cottage cheese, egg, and salt, pepper and nutmeg to taste; mix thoroughly.

Place a pancake on a heatproof plate, spread with some of the filling and cover with another pancake. Continue layering in this way, finishing with a pancake. Sprinkle with the cheese and cook in a preheated moderately hot oven, 190°C (375°F), Gas Mark 5, for for 30 to 40 minutes. Serve immediately, as a main dish.
Serves 4

Artichokes with Tomatoes

1 kg (2 lb) Jerusalem
    artichokes
salt and pepper
3 tablespoons olive oil
4 tomatoes, skinned
    and chopped
1 teaspoon chopped
    marjoram

Simmer the artichokes in boiling salted water for 20 minutes until almost cooked. Drain and cut into even-sized pieces.

Heat the oil in a pan, add the tomatoes, marjoram, artichokes, and salt and pepper to taste. Cover and simmer for 5 to 10 minutes. Transfer to a warmed dish. Serve immediately.
Serves 4

Aubergine Pie

1 kg (2 lb) aubergines
salt and pepper
200 ml (8 fl oz)
    olive oil
1 onion, chopped
1 clove garlic, crushed
500 g (1 lb) tomatoes,
    skinned and chopped
150 g (5 oz) natural
    low-fat yogurt
113 g (4 oz) cottage
    cheese
25 g (1 oz) grated
    Parmesan cheese

Slice the aubergines, sprinkle with salt and leave in a colander for 1 hour. Drain and pat dry with kitchen paper.

Heat 2 tablespoons of the oil in a pan, add the onion and fry until softened. Add the garlic and tomatoes and simmer, uncovered, for 5 to 7 minutes.

Mix the yogurt and cottage cheese together, adding salt and pepper to taste.

Heat the remaining oil in a frying pan and cook the aubergines on both sides until golden. Drain on kitchen paper.

Arrange a third of the aubergines in an ovenproof dish. Cover with half the tomato mixture, then top with half the yogurt mixture. Repeat the layers, finishing with aubergines.

Sprinkle with the Parmesan and cook in a preheated moderate oven, 180°C (350°F), Gas Mark 4, for 35 to 40 minutes. Serve immediately, as a main dish.

Serves 4

Courgette and Tomato Pie

3 tablespoons olive oil
2 onions, sliced
750 g (1½ lb)
    courgettes, sliced
2 cloves garlic, crushed
6 tomatoes, skinned
    and chopped
1 tablespoon tomato
    purée
salt and pepper
TOPPING:
750 g (1½ lb) potatoes,
    boiled and mashed
4 spring onions,
    finely chopped
2 tablespoons olive oil
4 tablespoons milk

Heat the oil in a pan, add the onions and courgettes and fry for 10 minutes, stirring occasionally. Add the garlic, tomatoes, tomato purée and salt and pepper to taste. Cover and simmer for 5 minutes, then turn into a 1.5 litre (2½ pint) ovenproof dish.

Beat the potatoes with the spring onions, oil, milk, and salt and pepper to taste. Spoon over the courgette mixture to cover. Cook in a preheated moderately hot oven, 200°C (400°F), Gas Mark 6, for 30 to 40 minutes until golden. Serve immediately, as a main dish.

Serves 4

Vegetable Curry

4 tablespoons oil
2 onions, sliced
2 teaspoons each
  ground coriander
  and turmeric
1 teaspoon curry
  powder
2 teaspoons chopped
  root ginger
2 cloves garlic, crushed
4 carrots, sliced
350 g (12 oz)
  courgettes, sliced
300 ml (½ pint) stock
salt and pepper
1 small cauliflower
50 g (2 oz) cashew
  nuts, roasted
150 g (5 oz) natural
  low-fat yogurt

Heat the oil in a large pan, add the onions and fry until softened. Add the spices and garlic and cook for a further 1 minute. Add the carrots and courgettes and fry for 2 to 3 minutes, stirring. Add the stock and salt and pepper to taste.

Cover and simmer for 10 minutes. Break the cauliflower into florets and cook for a further 10 minutes.

Stir in the nuts and yogurt and heat through gently. Serve with brown rice, as a main dish or an accompaniment.
Serves 4 to 6

Baked Courgette Soufflé

2 tablespoons oil
750 g (1½ lb) courgettes, grated
50 g (2 oz) margarine or butter
50 g (2 oz) wholemeal flour
200 ml (8 fl oz) milk
3 eggs, separated
salt and pepper
grated nutmeg
TOMATO SAUCE (optional):
25 g (1 oz) margarine or butter
500 g (1 lb) tomatoes, skinned and chopped
1 tablespoon chopped parsley
1 tablespoon chopped chives

Heat the oil in a large pan, add the courgettes and cook gently for 10 minutes, stirring occasionally.

Melt the fat in another pan, remove from the heat and stir in the flour. Add the milk and mix well. Return to the heat and slowly bring to the boil, stirring; simmer for 3 minutes. Cool slightly then add the egg yolks, courgettes, and salt, pepper and nutmeg to taste.

Whisk the egg whites until stiff and carefully fold into the mixture. Turn into a greased 1.2 litre (2 pint) ovenproof dish and place in a roasting pan containing 2.5 cm (1 inch) water. Cook in a preheated moderately hot oven, 190°C (375°F), Gas Mark 5, for 55 minutes to 1 hour.

Meanwhile, make the tomato sauce if using. Melt the fat in a pan and add the tomatoes, herbs, and salt and pepper to taste. Cook gently for 5 to 10 minutes, stirring occasionally. Sieve, or work in an electric blender until smooth; strain.

Serve immediately, as a main dish, starter or accompaniment, with the tomato sauce, if liked.
Serves 4 to 6

Potato Cake

500 g (1 lb) potatoes, grated
1 onion, chopped
2 tablespoons chopped parsley
1 egg, beaten
salt and pepper
2 tablespoons olive oil

Place the potatoes in a bowl with the onion, parsley, egg and salt and pepper to taste. Mix thoroughly.

Heat the oil in a 20 to 23 cm (8 to 9 inch) heavy frying pan. Add the potato mixture and pat lightly into a cake. Fry gently for 5 to 7 minutes until the underside is crisp and brown.

Slide onto a plate then invert back into the pan and fry the other side for 5 to 7 minutes until crisp and brown. Cut into wedges and serve immediately.
Serves 4

Chick Pea Curry

500 g (1 lb) chick
    peas, soaked
    overnight
3 tablespoons oil
2 onions, chopped
1 teaspoon chilli
    powder
2 teaspoons ground
    cumin
1 teaspoon ground
    coriander
2 teaspoons chopped
    root ginger
6 cardamoms, split
    and seeds removed
2 cloves garlic, crushed
500 g (1 lb) tomatoes,
    skinned and chopped
2 tablespoons tomato
    purée
salt and pepper
1 tablespoon chopped
    coriander or parsley

Drain the chick peas, place in a pan and cover with cold water. Bring to the boil and simmer for 2 hours. Drain and reserve the liquid.

Heat the oil in a large pan, add the onions and fry until softened. Add the spices and garlic and cook for a further 2 minutes. Add the tomatoes, tomato purée, chick peas, 300 ml ($\frac{1}{2}$ pint) of the reserved liquid, and salt and pepper to taste.

Cover and simmer gently for 1 hour or until the peas are tender. Sprinkle with the coriander or parsley. Serve as a main dish or accompaniment.
Serves 6

Lentil Stew

3 tablespoons oil
2 onions, chopped
4 carrots, sliced
4 celery sticks, sliced
1 clove garlic, crushed
1 bay leaf
500 g (1 lb) tomatoes
300 ml ($\frac{1}{2}$ pint) tomato
    juice
900 ml (1$\frac{1}{2}$ pints)
    water
300 g (10 oz) lentils
2 tablespoons chopped
    parsley
salt and pepper
chopped parsley to
    garnish

Heat the oil in a large pan, add the onions, carrots and celery and fry for 10 minutes until softened.

Skin the tomatoes and cut into quarters. Add to the pan with the remaining ingredients, seasoning with salt and pepper to taste. Cover and simmer for 50 minutes to 1 hour, stirring occasionally, until the lentils are tender.

Sprinkle with chopped parsley. Serve as a main dish with crusty wholemeal bread, or as an accompaniment.
Serves 4 to 6

Lentil Rissoles

2 tablespoons oil
1 onion, chopped
2 celery sticks, chopped
2 carrots, chopped
250 g (8 oz) lentils
600 ml (1 pint) water
1 teaspoon ground
   coriander
salt and pepper
2 tablespoons chopped
   parsley
175 g (6 oz) whole-
   meal breadcrumbs
2 tablespoons flour
1 egg, beaten
oil for shallow-frying
YOGURT SAUCE:
300 g (10 oz) natural
   low-fat yogurt
1 tablespoon chopped
   parsley
1 clove garlic, crushed
TO GARNISH:
parsley sprigs

Heat the oil in a pan, add the onion, celery and carrots and fry until softened. Add the lentils, water, coriander, and salt and pepper to taste. Bring to the boil, cover and simmer for 50 minutes to 1 hour, stirring occasionally. Mix in the parsley and one third of the breadcrumbs. Turn onto a plate to cool.

Using floured hands, shape the mixture into rissoles and coat with the flour. Dip into the beaten egg and coat with the remaining breadcrumbs.

Pour the oil into a frying pan to a depth of 5 mm ($\frac{1}{4}$ inch) and place over moderate heat. When hot, add the rissoles and fry until crisp and golden brown, turning once or twice.

To make the sauce, mix the yogurt, parsley and garlic together. Serve the rissoles garnished with parsley and accompanied by the sauce.

Serves 4

SALADS & DRESSINGS

Mushroom and Beanshoot Salad

350 g (12 oz) button
mushrooms,
quartered
6 tablespoons
Vinaigrette dressing
(see page 64)
250 g (8 oz) beanshoots
1 red pepper, cored,
seeded and finely
sliced

Place the mushrooms in a salad bowl,
add the dressing and toss well. Leave
to marinate for 1 hour, stirring
occasionally. Add the beanshoots and
pepper. Toss thoroughly before
serving.
Serves 6

Cauliflower and Watercress Salad

1 small cauliflower,
   broken into florets
salt
1 bunch of watercress
4 spring onions,
   chopped
5 tablespoons
   French dressing
   (see page 63)
1 tablespoon sesame
   seeds, roasted

Cook the cauliflower in boiling salted water for 3 minutes; drain and cool. Add the watercress, spring onions and dressing and toss thoroughly. Transfer to a salad bowl and sprinkle with the sesame seeds. Serve immediately.
Serves 6

Chinese Cabbage and Watercress Salad

1 small Chinese
  cabbage, shredded
1 bunch of watercress
4 oranges, segmented
5 tablespoons Mint and
  honey dressing (see
  page 64)

Put the cabbage, watercress and orange segments in a salad bowl. Pour in the dressing and toss well. Serve immediately.
Serves 6

Celery, Apple and Sesame Salad

1 head of celery,
  thinly sliced
4 red-skinned dessert
  apples, cored and
  thinly sliced
4 tablespoons
  Vinaigrette dressing
  (see page 64)
1 tablespoon sesame
  seeds, roasted

Place the celery and apple in a salad bowl. Pour in the dressing and toss well.
  Just before serving, mix in the sesame seeds.
Serves 6

Broad Bean Salad

500 g (1 lb) shelled
  broad beans
salt
juice of ½ lemon
1 teaspoon oil
3 tablespoons natural
  low-fat yogurt
4 tablespoons
  Mayonnaise (see
  page 62)
1 tablespoon chopped
  mixed herbs (parsley,
  thyme and chives)

Cook the beans in boiling salted water for 10 minutes, then drain and place in a bowl. Mix with the lemon juice and oil and leave to cool.
  Mix together the yogurt, mayonnaise and most of the herbs. Pour over the beans and mix well. Transfer to a salad bowl and sprinkle with the remaining herbs before serving.
Serves 4 to 6

Swedish Potato Salad

750 g (1½ lb) small
    new potatoes
salt
2 tablespoons French
    dressing (see
    page 63)
125 g (4 oz) cooked
    beetroot, diced
1 pickled dill
    cucumber, diced
5 tablespoons Yogurt
    dressing (see
    page 62)
1 tablespoon chopped
    dill

Scrub the potatoes clean but leave the skins on. Cook in boiling salted water until tender. Drain and mix with the French dressing while still warm. Leave to cool.

Add the beetroot, cucumber and yogurt dressing. Mix well, then transfer to a salad bowl. Sprinkle with the dill to serve.

Serves 6

Potato and Radish Vinaigrette

500 g (1 lb) small
    new potatoes
salt
4 tablespoons
    Vinaigrette dressing
    (see page 64)
4 spring onions, sliced
1 bunch of radishes,
    thinly sliced

Scrub the potatoes clean but leave the skins on. Cook in boiling salted water until tender. Drain well and mix with the dressing while still warm. Leave to cool.

Add the spring onions and radishes, mix well and transfer to a salad bowl to serve.

Serves 4

Mixed Bean Salad

125 g (4 oz) butter
    beans
125 g (4 oz) red
    kidney beans
125 g (4 oz) haricot
    beans
salt
125 g (4 oz) French
    beans, cut into
    2.5 cm (1 inch)
    lengths
6 spring onions,
    chopped
4 tablespoons French
    dressing (see page 63)
2 tablespoons chopped
    parsley

Soak the beans separately overnight. Drain and place in separate pans. Cover with cold water, bring to the boil and boil steadily for 15 minutes. Lower the heat, cover and simmer for 1 to 1½ hours, adding a little salt towards the end of cooking; drain.

Cook the French beans in boiling salted water for 7 to 8 minutes; drain. Place all the beans in a bowl and mix in the onions and dressing while still warm. Leave to cool.

Stir in the parsley and transfer to a salad bowl to serve. **Serves 6 to 8**

Coleslaw with Yogurt Dressing

½ medium white
  cabbage, finely
  shredded
2 celery sticks, chopped
2 dessert apples, cored
  and chopped
1 small onion, finely
  chopped
50 g (2 oz) sultanas
50 g (2 oz) walnuts,
  chopped
2 tablespoons chopped
  parsley (optional)
120 ml (4 fl oz)
  Yogurt dressing (see
  page 62)

Place all the ingredients in a salad bowl
and toss thoroughly to serve.
Serves 6

Brown Rice Salad

250 g (8 oz) brown
  rice
salt
3 spring onions, finely
  chopped
1 red pepper, cored,
  seeded and chopped
50 g (2 oz) raisins
50 g (2 oz) cashew
  nuts, roasted and
  chopped
2 tablespoons chopped
  parsley (optional)
6 tablespoons Soy
  sauce dressing (see
  page 64)

Cook the rice in boiling salted water
for 40 to 45 minutes until tender.
Rinse, drain well and cool.

  Place in a bowl and add the
remaining ingredients. Toss
thoroughly before serving.
Serves 6

Lentil and Tomato Salad

250 g (8 oz) lentils
  soaked for 1 hour
salt and pepper
6 tablespoons Tomato
  and garlic dressing
  (see page 62)
4 spring onions,
  chopped
4 tomatoes, skinned
  and chopped
2 celery sticks, sliced
1 tablespoon chopped
  parsley

Drain the lentils, place in a pan and cover with cold water. Add a little salt and simmer gently for 30 to 40 minutes until softened. Drain well and mix with the dressing while still warm. Leave to cool.

Add the remaining ingredients, seasoning with salt and pepper to taste. Mix together thoroughly.

Transfer to a salad bowl to serve.

Serves 6

Spinach and Mushroom Salad

250 g (8 oz) button
  mushrooms, sliced
4 tablespoons French
  dressing (see
  page 63)
250 g (8 oz) young
  spinach leaves
4 spring onions,
  chopped

Put the mushrooms in a bowl, add 3 tablespoons of the dressing and toss well. Leave to marinate for 1 hour, stirring occasionally.

Wash and thoroughly dry the spinach. Remove the thick centre stalks and tear the spinach leaves into a salad bowl. Add the marinated mushrooms, onions and remaining dressing. Toss well to serve.

Serves 4

Butter Bean and Cauliflower Salad

125 g (4 oz) butter
  beans, soaked
  overnight
salt
1 small cauliflower,
  broken into florets
125 g (4 oz) button
  mushrooms, sliced
6 tablespoons Green
  herb dressing (see
  page 63)

Drain the beans, place in a pan and cover with cold water. Bring to the boil and simmer for 1 hour or until softened, adding a little salt towards the end of cooking. Drain and cool.

Cook the cauliflower in boiling salted water for 3 minutes; drain and cool.

Place the beans, cauliflower and mushrooms in a salad bowl. Add the dressing and toss well. Serve immediately.

Serves 6 to 8

Mayonnaise

1 egg yolk
¼ teaspoon each salt,
  pepper and dry
  mustard
150 ml (¼ pint) olive
  oil
1–2 teaspoons cider
  vinegar

Beat the egg yolk and seasoning in a bowl. Add the oil drop by drop, beating constantly. As it thickens, add the oil in a steady stream. Add the vinegar and mix thoroughly.
Makes about 150 ml (¼ pint)

Tomato and Garlic Dressing

300 ml (½ pint)
  tomato juice
1 tablespoon lemon
  juice
1 clove garlic, crushed
2 tablespoons chopped
  chives
2 tablespoons olive oil
salt and pepper

Put all the ingredients in a screw-topped jar, adding salt and pepper to taste. Shake well to blend before serving.
Makes 300 ml (½ pint)

Yogurt Dressing

300 g (10 oz) natural
  low-fat yogurt
2 tablespoons lemon
  juice
1 clove garlic, crushed
salt and pepper

Place all the ingredients in a bowl, seasoning with ½ teaspoon salt and ½ teaspoon pepper. Mix together thoroughly. Store in an airtight container in the refrigerator.
Makes 300 ml (½ pint)

French Dressing

175 ml (6 fl oz)
  olive oil
4 tablespoons wine
  vinegar
1 teaspoon French
  mustard
1 clove garlic, crushed
1 teaspoon caster sugar
salt and pepper

Put all the ingredients in a screw-topped jar, adding salt and pepper to taste. Shake well to blend before serving.
Makes 250 ml (8 fl oz)

Green Herb Dressing

25 g (1 oz) parsley
15 g ($\frac{1}{2}$ oz) mint
15 g ($\frac{1}{2}$ oz) chives
1 clove garlic, chopped
150 g (5 oz) natural
  low-fat yogurt
120 ml (4 fl oz) oil
juice of $\frac{1}{2}$ lemon
salt and pepper

Remove the stalks from the parsley and mint. Place the leaves in an electric blender with the remaining ingredients, seasoning with $\frac{1}{2}$ teaspoon salt and $\frac{1}{4}$ teaspoon pepper. Blend for 2 to 3 minutes.

Store in an airtight container in the refrigerator. Shake well to blend before serving.
Makes 300 ml ($\frac{1}{2}$ pint)

Mint and Honey Dressing

2 tablespoons clear
  honey
4 tablespoons cider
  vinegar
3 tablespoons olive oil
1 tablespoon chopped
  mint
salt and pepper

Put all the ingredients in a screw-
topped jar, adding salt and pepper to
taste. Shake well to blend before
serving.
Makes 150 ml ($\frac{1}{4}$ pint)

Vinaigrette Dressing

175 ml (6 fl oz) olive
  oil
2 tablespoons cider
  vinegar
2 tablespoons lemon
  juice
1 teaspoon muscovado
  sugar
1 clove garlic, crushed
$\frac{1}{2}$ teaspoon mustard
2 tablespoons chopped
  mixed herbs (mint,
  parsley, chervil,
  chives and thyme)
salt and pepper

Put all the ingredients in a screw-
topped jar, adding salt and pepper to
taste. Shake well to blend before
serving.
Makes 250 ml (8 fl oz)

Soy Sauce Dressing

175 ml (6 fl oz) olive
  oil
4 tablespoons soy
  sauce
2 tablespoons lemon
  juice
1 clove garlic, crushed
1 cm ($\frac{1}{2}$ inch) piece
  root ginger, finely
  chopped
salt and pepper

Put all the ingredients in a screw-
topped jar, adding salt and pepper to
taste. Shake well to blend before
serving.
Makes 300 ml ($\frac{1}{2}$ pint)

DESSERTS

Raspberry and Hazelnut Crunch

75 g (3 oz) margarine
  or butter
125 g (4 oz) whole-
  meal breadcrumbs
75 g (3 oz) muscovado
  sugar
50 g (2 oz) hazelnuts,
  chopped and roasted
350 g (12 oz)
  raspberries

Melt the margarine or butter in a
frying pan, add the breadcrumbs and
cook until golden. Cool, then stir in
the sugar and hazelnuts.

Set aside 4 raspberries. Divide half
the remainder between individual
glass dishes and cover with half the
crumbs; repeat the layers.

Top with the raspberries and serve
chilled, with natural low-fat yogurt.
Serves 4

Watermelon with Honey

1 small watermelon
2 tablespoons clear
  honey
juice of $\frac{1}{2}$ lemon
2 tablespoons sherry
25 g (1 oz) flaked
  almonds, roasted

Scoop the flesh out of the watermelon, discarding the seeds, and cut into cubes.

Mix together the honey, lemon juice and sherry then fold in the melon. Chill for 1 hour.

Spoon into glasses and sprinkle with the almonds to serve.

Serves 4

Strawberry Cheesecake

50 g (2 oz) margarine
    or butter, melted
125 g (4 oz) digestive
    biscuits, crushed
25 g (1 oz) muscovado
    sugar
350 g (12 oz) curd
    cheese
4 tablespoons clear
    honey
150 g (5 oz) natural
    low-fat yogurt
grated rind and juice
    of 1 lemon
15 g (½ oz) gelatine,
    soaked in 3 table-
    spoons water
3 egg whites
250 g (8 oz)
    strawberries to
    decorate

Combine the margarine or butter, biscuit crumbs and sugar. Press the mixture over the base of a 20 cm (8 inch) loose-bottomed cake tin and place in the refrigerator for 20 minutes until firm.

Place the cheese in a bowl and mix in the honey, yogurt, lemon rind and juice. Beat until smooth. Place the soaked gelatine in a bowl over a pan of simmering water and stir until dissolved. Stir into the cheese mixture.

Whisk the egg whites until stiff, then fold lightly into the cheese mixture. Spoon over the biscuit base and chill for 2 to 3 hours until set.

Remove the cheesecake from the tin and arrange the strawberries on top.
Serves 6 to 8

Cheese and Yogurt Creams

227 g (8 oz) cream
    cheese
150 g (5 oz) natural
    low-fat yogurt
2 tablespoons clear
    honey
1 egg white
250 g (8 oz)
    strawberries

Place the cheese, yogurt and honey in a bowl and mix well. Whisk the egg white until fairly stiff then fold into the cheese mixture.

Line 6 heart-shaped moulds with muslin, spoon in the cheese mixture and smooth the tops. Place on a plate and leave to drain in the refrigerator for 3 to 4 hours. Turn out onto individual dishes and surround with strawberries.

Alternatively, spoon the cheese mixture into ramekin dishes, arrange the strawberries on top and chill until required.
Serves 6
NOTE: Other fresh soft fruit can be used in place of strawberries; e.g. raspberries, blackberries, cooked black-currants or redcurrants.

Mint and Apple Whip

750 g (1½ lb) cooking
    apples, peeled and
    cored
3 tablespoons clear
    honey
2 tablespoons water
6 large mint sprigs
5 tablespoons natural
    low-fat yogurt
2 egg whites
1 tablespoon
    muscovado sugar

Slice the apples into a pan and add the
honey, water and mint, reserving the
top leaves for decoration. Cover and
simmer for 10 to 15 minutes; discard
the mint. Sieve or work in an electric
blender until smooth. Leave to cool
then mix in the yogurt.

Whisk the egg whites until stiff,
then whisk in the sugar. Fold into the
apple mixture. Spoon into individual
dishes and decorate with the reserved
mint to serve.

Serves 4 to 6

Crunchy Hazelnut Ice

75 g (3 oz) wholemeal
  breadcrumbs
50 g (2 oz) hazelnuts,
  ground
175 g (6 oz)
  muscovado sugar
3 egg whites
300 g (10 oz) natural
  low-fat yogurt

Mix together the breadcrumbs, hazelnuts and 50 g (2 oz) of the sugar. Spread on a baking sheet. Place under a preheated hot grill for about 2 minutes until golden brown, stirring occasionally. Leave to cool.

Whisk the egg whites until stiff, then gradually whisk in the remaining sugar. Fold in the yogurt and breadcrumb mixture. Turn into a rigid freezerproof container. Cover, seal and freeze until firm.

Transfer to the refrigerator 30 minutes before serving to soften. Scoop into chilled glasses to serve.
Serves 6 to 8

Apricot Jelly

250 g (8 oz) dried
   apricots, soaked
   overnight
juice of $\frac{1}{2}$ lemon
1–2 tablespoons clear
   honey
15 g ($\frac{1}{2}$ oz) gelatine,
   soaked in 3 table-
   spoons water

Place the apricots in a pan with the
liquid in which they were soaked,
adding more water if necessary to
cover. Simmer for 20 to 30 minutes
until tender.

Place the apricots and liquid in an
electric blender with the lemon juice
and honey and blend until smooth.
Add water to make up to 750 ml
(1$\frac{1}{4}$ pints) if necessary.

Place the soaked gelatine in a bowl
over a pan of simmering water and stir
until dissolved. Stir into the apricot
mixture.

Pour into a 900 ml (1$\frac{1}{2}$ pint) ring
mould and chill until set.

Dip the mould quickly into hot
water to loosen and turn out onto a
serving dish.

Serves 4 to 6

Oatmeal and Yogurt Cream

40 g (1½ oz) blanched
   almonds, finely
   chopped
40 g (1½ oz) medium
   oatmeal
25 g (1 oz) muscovado
   sugar
grated rind and juice
   of ½ lemon
150 g (5 oz) natural
   low-fat yogurt
150 ml (¼ pint) double
   cream, whipped
1 tablespoon flaked
   almonds, roasted

Mix together the chopped almonds and
oatmeal. Spread on a baking sheet and
place under a preheated hot grill for
about 2 minutes, stirring frequently to
brown evenly. Leave to cool.

Mix the sugar with the lemon rind
and juice. Stir into the yogurt with the
almond mixture, then fold in the
cream.

Spoon into individual glass dishes
and chill until required. Decorate with
the flaked almonds to serve.

Serves 4

Prune Mousse

250 g (8 oz) dried
  prunes
50 g (2 oz) muscovado
  sugar
300 g (10 oz) natural
  low-fat yogurt
1 teaspoon lemon
  juice
15 g ($\frac{1}{2}$ oz) gelatine,
  soaked in 3 table-
  spoons water
150 ml ($\frac{1}{4}$ pint) double
  cream, whipped
25 g (1 oz) chopped
  walnuts to decorate

Cover the prunes with water, bring to
the boil and simmer for 20 minutes
until soft. Sieve, or work in an
electric blender with a little of the
cooking liquid until smooth; leave to
cool. Stir in the sugar, yogurt and
lemon juice.

Place the soaked gelatine in a bowl
over a pan of simmering water and
stir until dissolved. Cool slightly, then
fold into the prune mixture with the
cream. Pour into ramekins and chill
until set.

Decorate with the walnuts to serve.
Serves 6

Apricot Whip

250 g (8 oz) dried
  apricots, soaked
  overnight
300 g (10 oz) natural
  low-fat yogurt
2 egg whites
2 tablespoons
  muscovado sugar
1 tablespoon flaked
  almonds, roasted

Place the apricots in a pan with the
water in which they were soaked. Bring
to the boil and simmer for 20 minutes
until soft. Sieve, or work in an electric
blender with a little of the cooking
liquid until smooth. Leave to cool
then stir in the yogurt.

Whisk the egg whites until stiff,
then whisk in the sugar a little at a
time. Fold into the apricot mixture
and spoon into glasses. Sprinkle with
the almonds and chill until required.

Serves 6

Hazelnut Shortcake

HAZELNUT PASTRY:

75 g (3 oz) margarine
  or butter
50 g (2 oz) muscovado
  sugar
100 g (4 oz) whole-
  meal flour
75 g (3 oz) hazelnuts,
  ground and roasted
egg white for brushing
1 tablespoon chopped
  hazelnuts

FILLING:

500 g (1 lb) dessert
  apples, peeled,
  cored and sliced
2 tablespoons apple
  juice
50 g (2 oz) raisins
50 g (2 oz) sultanas
1 teaspoon ground
  mixed spice

Beat the fat and sugar together until soft. Stir in the flour and ground hazelnuts and mix to a firm dough. Turn onto a floured surface and knead lightly until smooth. Divide in half and roll each piece into a 20 cm (8 inch) round on a baking sheet. Brush one round with egg white and sprinkle with the chopped nuts.

Bake both rounds in a preheated moderately hot oven, 190°C (375°F), Gas Mark 5, for 10 to 15 minutes. Cut the nut-covered round into 8 sections while still warm. Transfer both rounds to a wire rack to cool.

Place the apples and juice in a pan, cover and cook gently for 15 minutes, stirring occasionally. Add the remaining ingredients and leave to cool.

Spread over the hazelnut round and arrange the cut triangles on top. Serve with natural low-fat yogurt.

Serves 8

Date and Apple Pancakes

PANCAKE BATTER:
*125 g (4 oz) whole-
  meal flour*
1 egg, beaten
300 ml (½ pint) milk
1 tablespoon oil
FILLING:
25 g (1 oz) margarine
*500 g (1 lb) dessert
  apples, peeled,
  cored and sliced*
*25 g (1 oz) muscovado
  sugar*
*½ teaspoon ground
  mixed spice*
*75 g (3 oz) dates,
  chopped*
TO FINISH:
*2 tablespoons clear
  honey*
*25 g (1 oz) flaked
  almonds, roasted*

Make and cook the pancakes as for
Spinach pancake layer (see page 44).

Melt the margarine in a pan and add
the apples, sugar, mixed spice and
dates. Cook gently, stirring frequently,
for 10 to 15 minutes until the apples
are tender.

Place a little of the filling on each
pancake, roll up and arrange in an
ovenproof dish. Warm the honey and
spoon over the pancakes to glaze. Bake
in a preheated moderate oven, 180°C
(350°F), Gas Mark 4, for 15 to
20 minutes until heated through.

Sprinkle with the almonds and
serve with natural low-fat yogurt.
Serves 4

Figgy Apples

4 large cooking apples,
  cored
1 tablespoon clear
  honey
75 g (3 oz) dried figs,
  chopped
1 tablespoon lemon
  juice
4 tablespoons apple
  juice

Make a shallow cut round the middle
of each apple.

Place the honey, figs and lemon juice
in a small pan and heat gently, stirring,
until mixed. Use to fill the apple
cavities, pressing down firmly.

Place in an ovenproof dish and pour
over the apple juice. Bake in a preheated moderate oven, 180°C (350°F),
Gas Mark 4, for 45 to 55 minutes until
soft. Serve hot with natural low-fat
yogurt.

Serves 4

Hot Fruit Salad

175 g (6 oz) dried
   apricots
125 g (4 oz) dried
   prunes
125 g (4 oz) dried
   figs
125 g (4 oz) dried
   apples
600 ml (1 pint) apple
   juice
2 tablespoons Calvados
   or brandy
25 g (1 oz) walnuts,
   coarsely chopped

Place the dried fruits in a bowl with
the apple juice and leave to soak
overnight.

Transfer to a saucepan and simmer
for 10 to 15 minutes. Turn into a glass
bowl and pour over the Calvados or
brandy. Sprinkle with the walnuts.
Serve immediately with natural low-
fat yogurt.
Serves 6

NOTE: This fruit salad can alternatively
be made in advance and served cold.

It can also be served, hot or cold,
with Sesame snaps (see page 84)
instead of walnuts and yogurt.

WHOLEGRAIN BAKING

Muesli Cake

175 g (6 oz) muesli
125 g (4 oz) molasses
  sugar
175 g (6 oz) sultanas
2 tablespoons malt
  extract
250 ml (8 fl oz) apple
  juice
2 cooking apples,
  peeled, cored and
  grated
175 g (6 oz) whole-
  meal flour
3 teaspoons baking
  powder
8 walnut halves

Place the muesli, sugar, sultanas, malt extract and apple juice in a mixing bowl and leave to soak for 30 minutes. Add the apple and flour, sift in the baking powder and mix together thoroughly.

Turn into a lined and greased 18 cm (7 inch) round cake tin and arrange the walnuts around the edge. Bake in a preheated moderate oven, 180°C (350°F), Gas Mark 4, for 1½ to 1¾ hours, or until a skewer inserted into the centre comes out clean. Leave in the tin for a few minutes, then turn onto a wire rack to cool.

Makes one 18 cm (7 inch) cake

Nutty Flapjacks

125 g (4 oz) margarine
120 ml (4 fl oz) clear
  honey
75 g (3 oz) muscovado
  sugar
250 g (8 oz) rolled
  oats
50 g (2 oz) walnuts,
  chopped

Melt the margarine with the honey and sugar in a pan. Stir in the oats and walnuts and mix thoroughly. Turn into a greased 18 × 28 cm (7 × 11 inch) shallow tin and smooth the top with a palette knife.

Bake in a preheated moderate oven, 180°C (350°F), Gas Mark 4, for 25 to 30 minutes.

Cool in the tin for 2 minutes, then cut into fingers. Cool completely before removing from the tin.
Makes 20

Banana and Walnut Slices

125 g (4 oz) margarine
or butter
125 g (4 oz) molasses
sugar
2 eggs
125 g (4 oz)
wholemeal flour
2 teaspoons baking
powder
2 bananas, mashed
125 g (4 oz) walnuts,
chopped

Cream the fat and sugar together until light and fluffy. Beat in the eggs, one at a time, adding a tablespoon of flour with the second egg. Fold in the remaining flour and baking powder with the bananas.

Spread the mixture evenly in a lined and greased 20 cm (8 inch) square shallow tin. Sprinkle with the walnuts and bake in a preheated moderately hot oven, 190°C (375°F), Gas Mark 5, for 20 to 25 minutes until the cake springs back when lightly pressed.

Leave in the tin for 2 minutes, then cut into 16 slices. Transfer to a wire rack to cool.

Makes 16 slices

NOTE: Chopped almonds or hazelnuts may be used in place of the walnuts.

Malted Chocolate Cake

175 g (6 oz) molasses sugar
2 eggs
120 ml (4 fl oz) corn oil
120 ml (4 fl oz) milk
2 tablespoons malt extract
175 g (6 oz) wholemeal flour
25 g (1 oz) cocoa powder
2 teaspoons baking powder
125 g (4 oz) curd cheese
75 g (3 oz) plain chocolate

Place the sugar, eggs, oil, milk and malt extract in a bowl and mix thoroughly. Add the flour, sift in the cocoa and baking powder and beat until smooth.

Divide the mixture between two lined and greased 18 cm (7 inch) sandwich tins and smooth with a palette knife.

Bake in a preheated moderate oven, 160°C (325°F), Gas Mark 3, for 25 to 30 minutes until the cakes spring back when lightly pressed. Turn onto a wire rack to cool.

Beat the cheese in a bowl until smooth. Melt the chocolate in a basin over a pan of hot water, add to the cheese and beat thoroughly.

Use half the mixture to sandwich the cakes together. Spread the remainder over the top of the cake and mark a swirl pattern, using a palette knife.
Makes one 18 cm (7 inch) cake

Sesame and Oat Biscuits

75 g (3 oz) rolled oats
50 g (2 oz) medium
  oatmeal
2 tablespoons sesame
  seeds, roasted
75 g (3 oz) molasses
  sugar
120 ml (4 fl oz) oil
1 egg, beaten

Place the oats, oatmeal, sesame seeds, sugar and oil in a mixing bowl. Stir well and leave to stand for 1 hour. Add the egg and mix thoroughly.

Place teaspoonfuls of the mixture well apart on a greased baking sheet and flatten with a palette knife.

Bake in a preheated moderate oven, 160°C (325°F), Gas Mark 3, for 15 to 20 minutes until golden brown. Leave to cool for 2 minutes then transfer to a wire rack to cool completely.
Makes about 25

Sesame Snaps

175 g (6 oz) medium
  oatmeal
50 g (2 oz) sesame
  seeds, roasted
6 tablespoons clear
  honey
6 tablespoons oil
50 g (2 oz) muscovado
  sugar

Place all the ingredients in a bowl and mix thoroughly. Press into a greased 20 × 30 cm (8 × 12 inch) Swiss roll tin and smooth the top with a palette knife.

Bake in a preheated moderate oven, 180°C (350°F), Gas Mark 4, for 20 to 25 minutes. Cool in the tin for 2 minutes, then cut into 24 squares. Cool completely before removing from the tin.
Makes 24

Malted Oat Fingers

120 ml (4 fl oz) oil
3 tablespoons malt
  extract
50 g (2 oz) muscovado
  sugar
125 g (4 oz) jumbo
  oats*
125 g (4 oz) rolled
  oats
2 tablespoons sesame
  seeds, roasted

Place the oil, malt extract and sugar, in a saucepan and heat gently. Add the remaining ingredients and mix thoroughly. Press into a greased 20 cm (8 inch) square shallow cake tin and smooth the top with a palette knife.

Bake in a preheated moderate oven, 180°C (350°F), Gas Mark 4, for 30 minutes.

Cool in the tin for 2 minutes then cut into 16 fingers. Cool completely before removing from the tin.
Makes 16
NOTE: If jumbo oats are unobtainable, omit and use 250 g (8 oz) rolled oats.

Digestive Biscuits

175 g (6 oz) whole-
  meal flour
50 g (2 oz) fine
  oatmeal
½ teaspoon salt
1 teaspoon baking
  powder
75 g (3 oz) margarine
25 g (1 oz) muscovado
  sugar
3–4 tablespoons milk
1 tablespoon sesame
  seeds

Mix the flour, oatmeal and salt together in a mixing bowl and sift in the baking powder. Rub in the margarine until the mixture resembles breadcrumbs, then stir in the sugar. Add the milk and mix to a firm dough.

Turn onto a floured surface and roll out thinly. Prick all over with a fork. Cut into 6 cm (2½ inch) rounds with a plain cutter. Brush with water and sprinkle with the sesame seeds.

Place on a greased baking sheet and bake in a preheated moderately hot oven, 190°C (375°F), Gas Mark 5, for 15 to 20 minutes. Transfer to a wire rack to cool.

Makes 20 to 24

Oat Cakes

350 g (12 oz) fine
  oatmeal
1 teaspoon salt
pinch of bicarbonate
  of soda
40 g (1½ oz)
  margarine
150 ml (¼ pint)
  boiling water

Place the oatmeal, salt and bicarbonate of soda in a mixing bowl.

Cut the margarine into pieces and place in a separate bowl. Pour over the water and stir until the margarine is melted. Add to the oatmeal and mix to a dough.

Turn onto a surface sprinkled with oatmeal and knead lightly until smooth. Dust with oatmeal and roll out very thinly into two 25 cm (10 inch) rounds. Cut each round into 8 sections and place on greased baking sheets.

Bake in a preheated cool oven, 150°C (300°F), Gas Mark 2, for 1 hour until crisp. Transfer to a wire rack to cool.

Reheat to serve if preferred. Spread with butter or cream cheese.
Makes 16

Date and Walnut Bread

125 g (4 oz)
  'Breakfast Bran'
75 g (3 oz) molasses
  sugar
125 g (4 oz) dates,
  chopped
50 g (2 oz) walnuts,
  chopped
300 ml (½ pint) milk
125 g (4 oz) whole-
  meal flour
2 teaspoons baking
  powder

Put the 'Breakfast Bran', sugar, dates, walnuts and milk in a mixing bowl. Stir well and leave for 1 hour. Add the flour, sift in the baking powder and mix together thoroughly.

Turn into a lined and greased 500 g (1 lb) loaf tin and bake in a preheated moderate oven, 180°C (350°F), Gas Mark 4, for 55 minutes to 1 hour, or until a skewer inserted into the centre comes out clean. Turn out onto a wire rack to cool.

Makes one 500 g (1 lb) loaf

Yogurt Scones

250 g (8 oz) whole-
  meal flour
½ teaspoon salt
½ teaspoon baking
  powder
50 g (2 oz) margarine
  or butter
1 tablespoon muscovado
  sugar
150 g (5 oz) natural
  low-fat yogurt
milk for brushing
sesame seeds for
  sprinkling

Place the flour and salt in a mixing bowl and sift in the baking powder. Rub in the fat until the mixture resembles breadcrumbs, then stir in the sugar. Add the yogurt and mix to a soft dough.

Turn onto a floured surface, knead lightly and roll out to a 2 cm (¾ inch) thickness. Cut into 5 cm (2 inch) rounds with a fluted cutter and place on a floured baking sheet. Brush with milk, sprinkle with sesame seeds and bake in a preheated hot oven, 220°C (425°F), Gas Mark 7, for 12 to 15 minutes. Transfer to a wire rack to cool.

Makes 12 to 14

Cheese and Sesame Scones
Sift in 1 teaspoon dry mustard and a pinch of cayenne pepper with the baking powder. Replace the sugar with 75 g (3 oz) grated cheese and 1 tablespoon sesame seeds.

Date and Nut Scones
Sift in ½ teaspoon ground cinnamon with the baking powder. Mix in 25 g (1 oz) chopped dates and 25 g (1 oz) chopped walnuts with the sugar.

Rye Bread

350 g (12 oz) rye
   flour
500 g (1 lb) whole-
   meal flour
2 teaspoons salt
25 g (1 oz) fresh
   yeast
450–600 ml ($\frac{3}{4}$–1 pint)
   warm water
2 tablespoons black
   treacle
2 tablespoons oil
milk for brushing
1 teaspoon caraway
   seeds

Mix the flours and salt together in a
bowl. Cream the yeast with a little of
the water and leave until frothy. Add
to the flour mixture with the remaining
water, treacle and oil and mix
thoroughly to a firm dough.

Turn onto a floured surface and
knead for 5 minutes until smooth and
elastic. Place in a clean bowl, cover
with a damp cloth and leave to rise in
a warm place for 2 hours, until
doubled in size.

Turn onto a floured surface and
knead for a few minutes. Shape into
2 oval loaves and place on greased
baking sheets. Prick with a fork in 8 or
9 places. Leave to rise in a warm place
for 1$\frac{1}{2}$ hours, until doubled in size.

Brush with milk and sprinkle with
caraway seeds. Bake in a preheated hot
oven, 220°C (425°F), Gas Mark 7, for
15 minutes. Lower the heat to 190°C
(375°F), Gas Mark 5, and bake for a
further 30 to 40 minutes until the
loaves sound hollow when tapped.
Cool on a wire rack.

Makes 2 loaves

NOTE: The proportion of rye flour to
wholemeal flour may be increased.

Wholemeal Bread

1.5 kg (3 lb) whole-
    meal flour
50 g (2 oz) fine
    oatmeal
1 tablespoon salt
25 g (1 oz) fresh yeast
900 ml–1.2 litres
    (1½–2 pints) warm
    water
2 tablespoons malt
    extract
2 tablespoons oil
2 tablespoons rolled
    oats

Mix the flour, oatmeal and salt together in a bowl.

Mix the yeast with a little of the water and leave until frothy. Add to the flour with the remaining water, malt extract and oil and mix to a smooth dough.

Turn onto a floured surface and knead for 8 to 10 minutes until smooth and elastic. Place in a clean bowl, cover with a damp cloth and leave to rise in a warm place for about 2 hours, until doubled in size.

Turn onto a floured surface, knead for a few minutes, then divide into 4 pieces. Shape and place in greased 500 g (1 lb) loaf tins. Brush with water and sprinkle with the oats.

Cover and leave to rise in a warm place for about 30 minutes, until the dough just reaches the top of the tins. Bake in a preheated hot oven, 220°C (425°F), Gas Mark 7, for 15 minutes.

Lower the temperature to 190°C (375°F), Gas Mark 5, and bake for a further 20 to 25 minutes until the bread sounds hollow when tapped. Turn onto a wire rack to cool.
Makes four 500 g (1 lb) loaves

Granary Stick

250 g (8 oz) granary
    flour
250 g (8 oz) whole-
    meal flour
1 teaspoon salt
15 g ($\frac{1}{2}$ oz) fresh yeast
300 ml ($\frac{1}{2}$ pint) warm
    water
1 tablespoon malt
    extract
1 tablespoon oil
cracked wheat
    for sprinkling

Mix the flours and salt in a bowl.

Cream the yeast with a little of the water and leave until frothy. Add to the flour with the remaining water, malt extract and oil; mix to a soft dough.

Turn onto a floured surface and knead for 5 minutes until smooth and elastic. Place in a clean bowl, cover with a damp cloth and leave to rise in a warm place for about 1½ hours until doubled in size.

Turn onto a floured surface and knead for a few minutes. Shape into a long stick and place on a greased baking sheet. Make slits slantwise along the length of the stick. Brush with water and sprinkle with cracked wheat. Cover and leave to rise in a warm place for about 30 minutes until almost doubled in size.

Bake in a preheated hot oven, 220°C (425°F), Gas Mark 7, for 25 to 30 minutes or until it sounds hollow when tapped. Cool on a wire rack.

Makes 1 granary stick

NOTE: If preferred the dough may be shaped into a round.

Herb and Onion Bread

750 g (1½ lb) whole-
  meal flour
2 teaspoons salt
15 g (½ oz) fresh yeast
450 ml (¾ pint) water
1 large onion, minced
1 tablespoon each
  chopped parsley,
  thyme and sage
1 tablespoon oil
1 tablespoon sesame
  seeds

Mix the flour and salt together in a bowl. Cream the yeast with a little of the water and leave until frothy. Add to the flour with the remaining water, the onion, herbs and oil and mix to a dough.

Turn onto a floured surface and knead for 8 to 10 minutes until smooth and elastic. Place in a clean bowl, cover with a damp cloth and leave to rise in a warm place for about 1½ hours, until doubled in size.

Turn onto a floured surface and knead for a few minutes. Form into a fairly wide roll and place on a greased baking sheet. Brush with water and sprinkle with the sesame seeds.

Cover and leave to rise in a warm place for about 30 minutes, until almost doubled in size.

Bake in a preheated hot oven, 220°C (425°F), Gas Mark 7, for 15 minutes. Lower the temperature to 190°C (375°F), Gas Mark 5, and bake for a further 20 to 25 minutes, until the bread sounds hollow when tapped. Turn onto a wire rack to cool.
Makes 1 loaf

INDEX

Acknowledgments

Photography by Paul Williams
Food prepared by Carole Handslip
Designed by Astrid Publishing Consultants Ltd